The Trials and Crucifixion of Jesus

By Bill Kincaid

Although this is a work of fiction, most of the characters in these pages existed, and the scenes depicted have been reconstructed as accurately as possible from data available to the author at the time the book was written. Various modern English translations of the *Bible* have been used as a basis for the scenes and dialogue, though additional dialogue has been invented from the author's imagination in order to make the scenes flow more smoothly.

Gethsemane

Jesus led his disciples to a place called Gethsemane, a garden and olive grove on the Mount of Olives where Jesus had gone in the past to pray. He said to his disciples, "Sit here, while I go over there and pray."

Taking with him his three closest disciples,[1] Jesus told them, "Stay here and keep watch with me."

Then he walked a little farther, fell on his face, and fervently prayed, "My soul is very sorrowful, even to death. Father, I know you can do all things. Therefore, if it is possible—if there is any other way by which my mission can be accomplished—please let this cup pass from me.

"I have seen men who have been nailed to crosses. I have heard their cries and curses as

---

[1] Peter, James and John.

they hang suspended between heaven and earth. But even worse is the prospect of taking on the sins of the world. I fear the cup of judgment. I shudder at the thought of being separated from you as part of that judgment. If that can be avoided, please let it be so. Nevertheless, it is not as I will, but rather your will that shall be done." Jesus' prayer was so extremely intense that bloody sweat appeared on his brow.[2]

When Jesus returned to the three disciples, he found that they were asleep.

"What?" Jesus remarked. "Could you not keep watch with me for even an hour? Watch and pray that you may not enter into temptation. The spirit indeed is willing, but the flesh is weak."

Jesus knew how weak the flesh would be. He knew that his disciples would flee in terror when the soldiers came to take him away. This would be the last time he would be with these

---

[2] This rather rare phenomenon, known as hematidrosis, occurs in cases of extreme psychic stress that causes the body to release chemicals that break down capillaries in the sweat glands, which then rupture and mix with sweat; hematidrosis also makes a person feel weak and dehydrated, and causes the skin to become fragile, tender, and extremely sensitive.

men who had lived and worked with him these past three years before they abandoned him. Yet he did not spend his time crying with them or even giving final instructions. Instead, he prayed for them.

"I pray for these men. Holy Father, protect them by the power of your name—the name you gave me—so that they may be one as we are one. I pray also for those who will believe in me through their message, that all of them may be one, Father, just as you are in me and I am in you. May they be brought to complete unity to let the world know that you sent me and have loved them even as you have loved me."

By the time Jesus finished praying, he had received the answer to his prayers. He had asked if there was any other way to successfully complete his mission. Now he knew there was no other way. God loved humanity—even with all its shortcomings, pride and sin—enough to take the sins of the world onto himself, become the perfect sacrifice for those sins, and complete his mission of redemption and love.

Trial Before the Sanhedrin

A large group of men bearing torches and armed with swords and clubs climbed up the limestone ridge toward Gethsemane. Judas Iscariot, who led the group, walked straight to Jesus, and said "Hail, Master!" Judas placed his right hand on Jesus' shoulder and kissed him on his cheek.

"Friend," said Jesus, "what brings you here?"

The armed detachment surrounded Jesus and grabbed him roughly. Simon Peter drew his sword and attempted to defend his master. Peter swung his sword mightily at Malchus, the High Priest's servant. Malchus dodged, but the sword cut off his right ear. Malchus made a startled cry and clutched his head. Blood oozed through his fingers. The soldiers holding Jesus released him as they turned toward Peter and drew their swords.

"Put away your sword," Jesus said to Peter, "for all who take up the sword will die by the sword." Jesus then picked up Malchus' ear, placed it back where it belonged, and instantly healed the wound. "Don't you realize that I could appeal to my Father, and he would immediately send me more than twelve legions of angels?" Jesus asked Peter. "But if I were to do that, how would the scriptures be fulfilled or my mission be accomplished? Shall I not drink the cup which my Father has given me? Though the way may be hard and painful, I must complete my mission."

Jesus turned and said to the elders and officers of the temple guard, "Have you come out with swords and clubs to capture me as if I were a robber? Day after day I sat in the temple teaching, and you did not seize me. Why do you do so now under cover of darkness?"

Peter, who had been backing up while Jesus was talking, turned and ran from the garden, followed closely by the other disciples, who ran for their lives. One of the soldiers grabbed hold of the robe worn by a young man named Mark who had been following the disciples. Mark twisted out of his robe and ran from the scene unclothed.

The band of soldiers bound Jesus and led him up the slope between the Upper City and the Tyropean to the Palace of Annas, the former high priest and father-in-law of Caiaphas, the current high priest. Annas then questioned Jesus about his disciples and his teaching.

"I have spoken openly to the world," replied Jesus. "I have continually taught in synagogues and in the temple, where all the Jews gather together, and I have said nothing in secret. Why ask me these questions? Ask those who have heard me what I told them, for they know what I have said."

Then one of the officers standing by him slapped Jesus' face with the palm of his hand and said, "Is that the way you answer the high priest?"

"If I have said anything wrong," replied Jesus, "bear witness to the wrong. But if I have answered correctly, why do you violate Jewish law by striking me?"

In the early morning about an hour or two after midnight, Annas had Jesus bound again and sent to Caiaphas at the palace of the high priest. Caiaphas had called an emergency meeting of the Great Sanhedrin, the Grand Council of the Jewish people.

Although the Sanhedrin was composed of seventy-one members who were appointed for life, the court could conduct business as long as it had a quorum of at least twenty-three members. The court sat in a semicircle with two clerks before them to record testimony and votes. Jesus and Caiaphas stood before the assembled Sanhedrin.

Then the chief priests and the whole council attempted to find witnesses who would testify against Jesus. Although they found several who were willing to testify, the witnesses' stories did not agree with one another on key points. The closest they could come was that two witnesses claimed that Jesus had said he could destroy the Temple of God and then rebuild it in three days—but even they contradicted each other on minor points.[3]

The high priest then said to Jesus, "Have you no answer to offer? What is this that these men are testifying against you?"

Jesus, however, remained silent and did not answer.

Caiaphas then said to Jesus, "I charge you on oath by the living God to tell us whether you are the Messiah, the Son of God." When a question was phrased in that manner to a loyal Jew, it was an offense not to answer.

"I AM," replied Jesus. "Hereafter, I tell you, you will see the Son of Man seated at the right hand of the Almighty and coming on the clouds of heaven."

The high priest dramatically tore his robes and said, "He has spoken blasphemy! What further need have we of witnesses? You have heard the blasphemy. What is your decision?"

"Death!" replied the council. "He deserves death!" Then they spat in Jesus' face and struck

---

[3]Under Jewish law, such contradictions could invalidate the witnesses' testimony.

him, saying, "Prophesy to us, Messiah! What is the name of the man who hit you?"

Jesus, however, did not respond to the attacks. Instead, he merely looked sorrowfully at the religious leaders, sighed and shook his head.

Meanwhile, Simon Peter had followed Jesus, though from a great distance. Peter entered the courtyard of the high priest's palace and sat down among the guards to await the outcome of Jesus' trial.

While Peter was sitting in the courtyard, a maid came up to him and said, "You were with Jesus, the Galilean, weren't you?"

"I don't know what you are talking about," Peter replied as he quickly stood up and looked around fearfully. He left the courtyard and went out onto the porch, where another maid pointed at him and told the bystanders, "This man was with Jesus, the Nazarene."

Again Peter denied it, adding with an oath, "I swear I don't know the man!"

Although Peter attempted to stand in the shadows away from other people, it was not long before several guards and bystanders surrounded Peter and said, "You are definitely one of Jesus' Galilean followers. Your accent gives you away."

Peter began to curse and to swear that he didn't know the man. While he was still speaking, a rooster crowed — and Peter remembered Jesus telling him, "Before the cock crows this day, you will already have denied three times that you even know me." To make matters worse, when Peter looked around to see if anyone else was watching him, he saw Jesus looking sorrowfully at him while being led from one of the rooms.

The sudden realization that he had failed as a disciple hit Peter like a thunderbolt. He prided himself on his loyalty and love for Jesus, whom he considered to be his Lord and Master. Worse, he had loudly and proudly proclaimed that even if everyone else deserted Jesus, he would stand firm. After all, he was Peter, the rock. His faith would not waiver. But instead of standing tall, he had fallen short. The very thing he had sworn he would never do was exactly what he had just done. He had let his Master down. He had let the disciples down. He had failed to live up to even his own standards for himself. Instead of being the leader he had claimed to be, Peter had failed miserably. He stumbled from the palace, weeping bitterly.

Peter was so blinded by his tears that he did not notice the two men who passed him as they entered the courtyard he had just vacated. Both men wore garments with the wide fringes that indicated they were Pharisees, and both wore the headdresses that marked them as being members of the Sanhedrin. Both men walked briskly to the chamber in which the trial of Jesus had taken place.

"What is going on in here?" demanded one of the men.

"Oh, Nicodemus, Nicodemus," responded Matthias. "The high priest called an emergency meeting of the Sanhedrin."

"Why were we not notified of the meeting?" Nicodemus asked.

"Because of the emergency nature of the meeting, there was not time for everyone to be contacted," Matthias answered. "It would have taken too long to get word to Joseph in

Arimathea, for example," he added, glancing at the second man.

"Not too long," Joseph commented, "since I was spending the night at Nicodemus' house. If you had contacted him, you would also have reached me."

"Well, it wasn't really necessary," Matthias said. "We already had more than the twenty-three members necessary to conduct a trial."

"A trial?" Joseph asked. "A trial of whom?"

"Why, a trial of Jesus of Nazareth. He admitted under oath that he was the Messiah, the Son of God. The Sanhedrin naturally found him guilty of blasphemy and has determined that he deserves to be put to death."

"A trial *at night — during the Passover?*" Nicodemus asked incredulously. "That is highly illegal!"

"Oh, you worry too much, Nicodemus. If it had really been illegal, I am sure neither the high priest nor the council would have done it. However, what's done is done. Even now Jesus is being led to Pontius Pilate to be charged according to Roman law." Matthias then smiled benignly and turned away.

Sensing that his friend was about to explode in wrathful fury, Joseph took Nicodemus by the arm and quietly whispered in his ear, "Before you say anything else, look around you and observe who is here. Only those members of the Sanhedrin who are committed to the high priests' opposition to Jesus are present. Apparently none of the more moderate members or those who would insist that we must follow our own law were notified. We would have had no notice of these proceedings ourselves if Bartholomew had not contacted us with the news that Jesus had been arrested. I suggest we quietly go to more private chambers, where we can draft a formal opposition to these proceedings."

"What good would that do?"

"We may be able to get notice to the other members of the Great Sanhedrin, and to persuade them to reconsider and to rescind the findings of this illegal trial. Or, if that doesn't work, we may be able to present the information to the Romans or even to the people who have gathered for the Passover."

"Very well, Joseph. As you say, the group that is currently assembled does not seem to be inclined to respect our own Jewish legal requirements. However, it may be prudent to set these matters out for others to consider."

When the two men had found a private chamber well removed from the others, Joseph began taking notes. Nicodemus paced back and forth as he collected his thoughts.

"First," said Nicodemus, "our own Jewish law requires that there can be no trials during the Passover, during the night, or on the eve of the Sabbath. All of those requirements have been violated. Further, it appears that the high priests acted as both prosecutors and as judges, which is highly improper. Our law does not allow any man who is concerned or interested in a matter under adjudication to even sit on the court — much less to act as prosecutor or judge."

"Matthias said Jesus' conviction was based upon his own sworn testimony," Joseph said. "Isn't that also irregular?"

"Right you are, Joseph. Our law does not permit forced self-incrimination, nor does it allow a person to be condemned merely on his own testimony.

"It also appears that they conducted this 'trial' as a capital case," Nicodemus continued. "Our law does not allow a capital case to be tried in one sitting; it must carry over to a second day in order to accomplish the rules of justice."

Nicodemus paused to allow Joseph to catch up with his notes and to flex his hand. When Joseph again picked up his stylus, Nicodemus continued, "Furthermore, if the court votes for conviction, the court must adjourn without passing sentence. Only after it has reconvened the following day and the evidence is again reviewed may another vote be taken and sentence be passed."

"Is that the reason we are forbidden to conduct a criminal trial on the day preceding the Sabbath?" Joseph asked.

"Yes," replied Nicodemus, "since the follow-up trial could not be had on that day. There were additional irregularities as well. According to Bartholomew, the arrest of Jesus was apparently brought about through the actions of a traitor who had been hired by the high priests or possibly by the court that would be passing judgment on Jesus. The Sanhedrin does not have authority to instigate charges, but is only supposed to investigate charges brought before it. Yet in this instance the court itself formulated the charges. Caiaphas presented the charges and served as prosecutor—another violation—even though as high priest he was also the presiding judge."

"I don't remember having any prior trials here at the home of the high priest," Joseph commented.

"Good point, Joseph. This night-time *'trial'* was conducted at the high priest's palace rather than in the *Liscat Haggazith*[4]. Jewish law requires that there be an exhaustive search into the facts presented by any witnesses, but apparently Jesus was permitted no defense. There were probably other irregularities or illegalities that we might have noted had we been present, but this partial assembly of the

---

[4] The hall of polished stone where the Sanhedrin was supposed to conduct its trials and deliberations

Sanhedrin was apparently carefully chosen to validate the high priest's predetermined verdict rather than to conduct a trial according to Jewish laws of justice."

Pilate

Shortly after daybreak on the fourteenth day of Nisan in the year 3790[5], the chief priests and elders delivered Jesus to Pontius Pilate, the Roman governor of Judea. After Herod the Great died and his son Archelaus was banished, Rome had appointed a series of governors to rule over Judea. Pilate was Rome's military procurator, and his ultimate responsibility was to the emperor himself.

Although Pilate normally stayed at his official residence in Caesarea, it was his custom to go to Jerusalem during Passover in order to quell any uprisings that might occur. While in Jerusalem, Pilate stayed at the Praetorium, the

---

[5] i.e., April 7, 30.

former palace of Herod the Great that was located on high ground in the northwestern portion of the Upper City, the newer portion of Jerusalem where most of the homes of wealthier citizens were located.

The chief priests and elders did not actually enter the Praetorium, since entering such a Gentile structure could cause them to be ceremonially unclean or defiled, which would mean they would be unable to partake of the Passover. Although it galled Pilate to leave the Roman fortress in order to meet with men he considered to be religious fanatics, he was nevertheless enough of a political realist to follow the most expedient course of action and do what had to be done. He therefore went out to the Jewish religious leaders and asked, "What charge do you bring against this man?"

"If he were not a criminal," they replied, "we would not have handed him over to you."

Pilate examined the accused with the keen eyes of a trained soldier. The man before him had no weapons and apparently no confederates or accomplices. The tall, thin governor had seen many criminals and insurrectionists and prided himself on being a good judge of character. This man did not appear to be a vicious troublemaker, though he did have an aura of authority about him.

"Take him and judge him according to your own law," Pilate said dismissively.

"We are not allowed to put anyone to death," replied Caiaphas, who then accused Jesus of several crimes: "We found this man perverting our nation and forbidding people to pay taxes to Caesar, saying that he himself is the Messiah, the king of the Jews.[6]"

---

[6] The Sanhedrin had convicted Jesus of blasphemy (claiming to be God or making oneself equal to God) rather than perverting the nation, forbidding people to pay taxes to Caesar, or claiming to be a king. Although blasphemy was an offense that was punishable by death under Jewish law, and although the Sanhedrin had the legal right to pronounce the death sentence, the Romans had restricted that right when they conquered Palestine. The Romans reserved for themselves the right to carry out a death sentence for all offenses other than threatening the sanctity of the Jewish temple. Since the Jewish leaders had been unable to find Jesus guilty of threatening to destroy the temple, control over Jesus was surrendered to the Romans--and the accused had to be found guilty of a capital offense according to Roman law. Indeed, Rome had removed Annas from his office as high priest because he had violated that restriction. Thus, when the Jewish religious authorities turned Jesus over to Pilate for sentencing, they did not say he had been found guilty of blasphemy, which would not have concerned the Romans, but rather claimed that he was guilty of committing treason, sedition, and other related offenses.

Since these were potentially serious charges that Pilate could not safely ignore, and since there was something about the accused man's bearing that was both strange and compelling, he decided to examine the prisoner more fully, but away from the Jews who were seeking the man's death. Pilate went back into the Praetorium and had Jesus brought to him. He studied Jesus for a few moments and then remarked sarcastically, "*You* are the King of the Jews?"

"Are you saying this of your own accord?" replied Jesus. "Or did others say this to you about me?"

"Am I a Jew?" snapped Pilate. "Your own nation and the chief priests have handed you over to me. What have you done?"

A slight smile tickled the corners of Jesus' mouth. *What had he done?* Over the past three years he had primarily spent his waking hours preaching, teaching, healing and helping people. When asked a similar question by messengers from John the Baptist, Jesus had replied, "The blind receive their sight, the lame walk, lepers are cleansed, the deaf hear, the dead are raised up to life again, and the poor have the gospel preached unto them."

True, those were all important accomplishments — but they would probably hold little interest for Pilate. Jesus therefore responded, "My kingdom is not of this world. If my kingdom were of this world, my servants would have fought to keep me from being handed over to the Jews. But my authority as king is not of earthly origin."

"Are you indeed a king?" Pilate asked.

"You are right in saying that I am a king," replied Jesus. "For this purpose I was born, and for this cause I have come into the world, to bear witness to the truth. Those who love the truth listen to my voice."

"What is truth?" muttered Pilate to himself. If Jesus' kingdom was not of this world, it would not be in conflict with Caesar's empire. Pilate had heard enough to confirm his initial conclusion that this man was harmless. He then went out to the Jews and announced, "I do not find this man guilty of any crime." Pilate's public verdict that Jesus was not guilty angered the Jewish religious leaders, who then began to accuse Jesus of many other things in an effort to get Pilate to reconsider.

"Have you no answer to offer?" Pilate asked Jesus. "Didn't you notice how many charges they have brought against you?"

But Jesus made no reply, which astonished Pilate.

The chief priest then grew more insistent, saying, "This man has been stirring up the people with his teachings, causing disturbances all the way from where he started in Galilee to here."

"Is he a Galilean?" asked Pilate.

"He is," Caiaphas answered.

Pilate turned to his steward and commanded, "Have a detachment of soldiers take the prisoner to Herod Antipas.[7] He's staying at the Palace of the Maccabees here in Jerusalem during the Passover."

When Herod Antipas was informed that Roman soldiers had brought Jesus of Nazareth to him, he responded, "Ah, excellent. I have

---

[7] Galilee was in Herod Antipas' jurisdiction.

heard much about him and am glad to finally see him in person."

Turning to his guests, Herod announced, "We may have a chance for better entertainment than these poor jugglers have provided. I have just been informed that the Romans have brought me Jesus of Nazareth. Perhaps he will show us one of his famous miracles."

Flanked by two guards, Jesus was brought before Herod Antipas, who studied him for about a minute before remarking, "So you are the famous miracle man of Galilee."

Jesus merely looked at Herod without responding.

"Is it true you raised people from the dead and fed thousands of people with very little food?"

Jesus made no response.

"At least Moses put on a show for Pharaoh. Can't you do the same for us?"

No response.

A commotion signaled the arrival of the chief priests and scribes, who demanded to be taken to Herod.

"Sire," said Caiaphas, "this man is a threat to your throne, since he claims to be a king."

"A king?" chuckled Herod. "Him?"

"Yes, Sire. He claims to be the Messiah spoken of by the prophets."

Turning back toward Jesus, Herod remarked, "You heard the priest. What have you to say in your defense?"

Again Jesus said nothing.

"He also encouraged people not to pay their taxes!" added Matthias.

"No taxes?" Herod quipped to his guests. "Now this is really getting serious!"

Still Jesus made no response.

After silently watching Jesus for a couple of minutes, Herod growled, "Say something, damn you."

No response.

"Maybe what I need is another miracle man to make this first one come alive and say or do something."

Jesus continued standing respectfully in front of Herod without answering.

"Enough of this!" Herod declared as he summoned one of his slaves and ordered,

"Fetch one of my older royal robes and bring it here."

When the slave returned with the robe, Herod Antipas ordered one of his soldiers to put it on Jesus. Herod and his guests finally had their entertainment as the soldiers gave mock allegiance to Jesus.[8] He then had Jesus returned to Pilate's custody.

Pilate called together the chief priests and rulers and said to them, "You brought this man to me as one who is misleading the people. After examining him before you, I have not found this man guilty of your charges against him. Nor did Herod, for he sent him back to me. This man has done nothing deserving of death. I will therefore give him a flogging and release him."

Thus Pilate announced a second verdict of not guilty, but this time he coupled his verdict with a sentence of flogging for the man he had just declared innocent of all charges. Pilate

---

[8] By mocking Jesus in the presence of the religious leaders, Herod hoped to curry their favor—but he refrained from passing sentence on a rabbi who was popular with the people and who had a reputation for being able to work mighty miracles.

realized that it was because of their envy that the religious leaders had condemned Jesus, and he hoped that the sight of a bruised, bleeding and broken man would mollify the Jewish leaders enough to end the charade. Then the governor thought of another possible solution.

It was the custom of Pilate at the time of the Passover festival to release one prisoner to the Jews. Although he generally allowed the Jews to choose the prisoner, Pilate seized upon this custom as a means of getting out of his dilemma. He narrowed the choice to two men: Jesus and a murderer and insurrectionist named Barabbas. After all, he reasoned, who would not choose a great teacher over a notorious criminal?

But Pilate had not correctly evaluated how deeply the religious leaders feared and hated Jesus. The chief priests and elders persuaded the mob to ask for Barabbas and to demand the death of Jesus. The governor responded by saying to them again, "Which of the two do you want me to release to you?"

"Barabbas!" they answered.

"Then what shall I do with Jesus, who is called Messiah?" asked Pilate.

"Let him be crucified!" the crowd shouted.

Pilate's clever compromise had backfired. Instead of freeing himself, the governor had painted himself into a corner. Stunned and almost in a state of shock, he cried back to the people, "Why? What crime has he committed?"

But the mob shouted all the more, "Let him be crucified." The people then began chanting, "Crucify! Crucify! Crucify him!"

Pilate realized with horror that a riot was developing, which he could not afford at this stage of his career. He had been appointed to his position by Sejanus, who had become the *de facto* leader of Rome when Emperor Tiberius retired to the resort island of Capri four years earlier. But when Tiberius discovered that Sejanus was responsible for killing the emperor's son, Sejanus was executed, and his friends and political appointees were in danger of similar treatment.

Pilate, who had been both a friend and a political appointee of Sejanus, did not want Tiberius to have any excuse for ending his career—or his life. He took a basin of water and symbolically washed his hands in front of the people. "I am washing my hands of this affair," he said. "I am innocent of the blood of this just and righteous person. The responsibility is yours."

"May his blood be on us and on our children!" the people responded.

Then Pilate released Barabbas to them, and handed Jesus over to his soldiers to be whipped and crucified. Jesus was flogged with a Roman scourge[9], which consisted of leather straps into which pieces of sheep bone and metal had been woven, and weighted with lumps of lead at the tip of each thong. Stripped to the waist, Jesus was tied to a pillar in a stooping position that fully exposed his back.

Jesus arched his back in agony as the bits of bone and metal tore into his flesh. Each lash of

---

[9] Probably a *flagrum*, a whip with several long leather tails.

the scourge ripped his body, lacerating both the skin and muscles. Since Jesus' skin was especially sensitive and fragile as a result of the hematidrosis he had suffered a few hours earlier in the Garden of Gethsemane, the brutal Roman flogging was especially destructive. Soon Jesus' back was a mass of quivering ribbons of bleeding flesh—and still the flogging continued. Jesus gasped with pain as one of the metal weights crashed into his ribs. The jeering soldiers who were watching cheered as the sound reverberated around the courtyard.

The pain was so intense that Jesus found it necessary to direct all his thoughts to repeatedly muttering through clinched teeth, "Father, forgive them. Please don't hold this to their account. Forgive them. Forgive them." By the time the scourging ended after thirty-nine lashes, all of Jesus' back was totally shredded and laid open so that even his bones, sinews and bowels were exposed. His right lung had collapsed, and there was profuse bleeding into his chest cavity, and then down his legs. Jesus had lost enough blood that his body was beginning to experience hypovolemic shock.[10]

The soldiers then took the royal robe Herod had placed on Jesus as part of his mockery, and they placed it about his bleeding frame. Someone had braided a crown of thorns, and this was pressed down on Jesus' head. The sharp thorns cut into his flesh until the blood flowed freely from the wounds. The soldiers then placed a reed in Jesus' right hand, and they all kneeled down before him in mock subjection, shouting, "Hail, King of the Jews!" Then they spat on him, yanked the reed from him, and struck him on the head with it. When the soldiers finally finished mocking Jesus, they led him back to the governor.

Pilate addressed the mob one more time, saying, "Behold, I am bringing him out to you so that you may know that I find him guilty of

---

[10] Hypovolemic shock is caused by losing large amounts of blood. The victim's heart races in an effort to pump blood that isn't there; his blood pressure drops, which causes the victim to faint or collapse; his kidneys stop producing urine, and the body craves fluids to replace the lost volume of blood.

no crime." The bruised and bleeding Jesus, still wearing the crown of thorns and royal robe, slowly shuffled out before the people. "Behold, here is the man!" said Pilate.

When the chief priests and the officers saw him, they shouted, "Crucify him! Crucify him!"

"Take him and crucify him yourselves," said Pilate, "for I do not find him guilty of any crime."

"We have a law," answered Caiaphas, "that says he should die because he claimed to be the Son of God."

When Pilate heard this, he became even more alarmed. He took Jesus back inside the Praetorium and asked him, "Who *are* you? Where did you come from?"

When Jesus did not answer him, Pilate said, "Aren't you going to speak to me? Don't you know that I have the authority to release you, and the authority to crucify you?"

"You would have no authority at all over me had it not been given to you from above," replied Jesus. "Therefore, he who handed me over to you is guilty of the greater sin."

Hearing this, Pilate renewed his efforts to release Jesus. Pilate first consulted with Julius, the governor's chief advisor, who gave the governor a summary of the information the Romans had collected regarding Jesus: He was a religious teacher who seemed to have unusual powers. He had fed thousands of people with virtually no food — and the reports claimed he had ended up with more food than when he had started. He had healed large numbers of people and had even restored life to several dead people. None of the soldiers or Roman spies reported any insurrection or other criminal acts worth noting with the possible exception of a notation that one of Jesus' disciples had been a Zealot prior to joining up with Jesus.

A man who can feed thousands of people with virtually no food and who can heal the suffering and misery of the masses would be a powerful ally, Pilate thought. *Or a dangerous enemy!*

Pilate reread a note he had received from his wife: "Have nothing to do with that righteous man, for last night I suffered greatly in a dream because of him." *What is it about this man that even causes my wife to have disturbing dreams? I wish it were that simple to just have nothing to do with this entire affair. A religious leader with unusual powers . . . What if he actually is the son of the Jews' God?*

Pilate next met with Odaenathus, a Roman attorney hired by Joseph of Arimathea. Although Odaenathus admitted that as military governor, Pilate was not required to follow particular rules and forms of law, he pointed out that Pilate also had the right and power to apply either the law of the forum[11] or the law of the community.[12]

After presenting to Pilate the ways the members of the Sanhedrin had broken their own Jewish law in their trial of Jesus, Odaenathus suggested that Pilate follow the criminal procedure generally used in capital cases tried in Rome. This would require an initial hearing to be held to determine which prosecutor should present the case, and to review the charges against the accused.

---

[11] In this case, Roman law.

[12] Jewish law.

If it was determined that there was enough evidence against the accused to warrant a trial, an indictment would be issued and presented to the tribunal, which would then set a date for the trial. As Odaenathus pointed out, this would allow the governor to get beyond the Passover crowds and the current mob that was obviously being controlled by the jealous Jewish religious leaders. The trial could even be held in a site more likely to produce a just result than in Jerusalem.

Pilate listened and privately agreed. When he attempted to implement that course of action, however, Caiaphas shouted, "You are not a friend of Caesar! Everyone who sets himself up as a king proclaims treason against Caesar."

The other priests took up the chant of "You're not a friend of Caesar."

Just as a card shark might save back an "ace in the hole" or the controlling trump card so that it could be used when needed in the decisive moment, so had the Jewish religious leaders reserved their strongest argument or threat for this moment. "A friend of Caesar" was a title bestowed upon those who acted in the emperor's best interests. Thus, by suggesting that Pilate would not be loyal to Caesar if he either released Jesus or failed to crucify him, they were threatening to report Pilate's actions to Tiberius Caesar, who had a reputation for sometimes reacting impulsively rather than considering all the facts, evidence and context.

The religious leaders had successfully appealed to Rome previously, and the memory of Tiberius' wrath on those occasions still burned in Pilate's mind. He knew his own life could be endangered if Tiberius Caesar learned that his governor had refused to execute a man who claimed to be a *king* in opposition to Caesar's claims as emperor. When Pilate heard these words, he brought Jesus out and sat down on the cobalt blue curule judgment seat at a place called The Pavement, which was an elevated platform of stone on which the *bema*[13] rested. Pilate said to the Jews, "Behold, your king!"

---

[13] The judgment seat.

"Away with him; away with him; crucify him!" shouted the angry mob, jabbing and shaking their fists in the air.

"Shall I crucify your king?" asked Pilate.

"We have no king but Caesar," answered Caiaphas. The mob echoed his words.

Then Pilate summoned Longinus, the centurion in charge of the crucifixion detail of soldiers from the famous Roman Twelfth Legion, and Longinus led Jesus away.

Judas Iscariot had been watching from the shadows as the drama unfolded. He had seen the farce of a trial, watched Pilate vainly seek some way to free Jesus without inciting a riot, and listened as sentence was ultimately passed.

The scene in the Garden of Gethsemane kept replaying itself in Judas' mind. When he had greeted Jesus with a kiss, Jesus had gently asked him, "Friend, what brings you here?" Jesus' sorrowful eyes seemed to be asking, "Friend, why have you done this?"

Why had he done it, anyway? At the time it had seemed to make sense to Judas. He had hoped to force the Rabbi's hand—force him to finally take the decisive action needed to declare himself as the long awaited Messiah and establish his everlasting kingdom on earth. After all, any man who can multiply food to feed the multitudes, heal the sick and dying, effortlessly control the storms and forces of nature, and even raise the dead back to life again surely has the power to overcome the Romans. He undoubtedly had the power to deflect enemy arrows, to feed and heal his troops, and even to restore life to those who fell in battle. His army would be invincible!

Jesus, however, seemed reluctant to take that decisive step. True, he had revealed himself as being the Messiah—but only to his disciples or in other private conversations. What was needed was something to ignite the spark. After Lazarus' resurrection, the witnesses were ready to proclaim Jesus as the promised Messiah and to follow him wherever he would lead them—but Jesus had merely disappeared into the house.

Judas had thought long and hard about what it would take to get Jesus to publicly declare himself as the Messiah. Judas eventually concluded that his most promising option would be to turn Jesus over to the jealous Jewish religious leaders. Granted, there were some risks involved, but Judas believed that the masses that had flocked to Jesus on Palm Sunday would surely rally to his defense and would unite behind Jesus in a popular groundswell of support that would proclaim Jesus as the long-awaited Messiah who would deliver his people from Roman oppression.

But Judas' plan had gone horribly wrong. Instead of uniting behind Jesus, the mob united against him. Instead of overthrowing the Roman oppressors, Jesus was about to be crucified by them. And most maddening of all was that Jesus was allowing it to happen! He did not summon the armies of heaven or even call upon the forces of nature. Time and again Judas had seen Jesus restore dead people to life. Now this one who had power over life and death was willingly walking to his own death. *Like a lamb being led to be slaughtered,* thought Judas. *It's maddening! Pointless! Insane!*

Judas bitterly turned from the scene and absentmindedly caressed the purse containing the thirty pieces of silver given to him by the jealous religious leaders. When he received the money, Judas thought of it as a bonus for ingeniously prompting the Rabbi to lead the movement that would overthrow the Roman dogs. Now the coins mocked him each time he heard them jingle. Judas had betrayed the Rabbi for the price of a slave! Betrayed! Only a trusted friend can truly betray someone. Judas had violated his Master's trust. What use had he for blood money?

Judas was filled with remorse and brought back the thirty pieces of silver to the priests and elders at the temple. Judas kneeled down before them, held out the money, and said, "I have sinned by betraying innocent blood."

"What is that to us?" Annas replied. "That is your affair."

Judas looked at the priests through eyes devoid of any hope. The priests were caretakers of an empty religion also devoid of hope and meaning. They went through an empty charade of rituals and pompous ceremonies. *For what purpose? What meaning? The only man who had ever given meaning to life was the one Judas had betrayed.* Well, Jesus had warned that it would have been better for the man who betrayed him if he had never been born. How true were those words—and how they now cut Judas to the bone.

Judas threw the silver down in the courtyard[14] and ran away, howling his dismay like a madman. Perhaps he was a madman. It *would* have been better if he had never been born. Not only was he a failure, but he was also a traitor to his Master. If anyone ever remembered Jesus in the future, they very likely would also remember that he had been betrayed by Judas Iscariot. That was not the way Judas wanted to be remembered, but there was nothing he could do now to rectify his actions.

Judas stumbled blindly down the dusty streets of Jerusalem. Where could he go?

---

[14] The priests picked up the silver coins and commented, "It is unlawful to put this into the temple treasury, since it is the price of blood." After discussing their options, they eventually used the money to purchase the "potters' field"—so named because its clay was used by potters to make jars and pots—to use as a burial place for strangers and paupers. Because the land was purchased with Judas' blood money, the land became known as the Field of Blood.

Certainly not back to the disciples with whom he had lived these past three years. He couldn't even return to his family after what he had done. Instead of being honored as the one who helped lead Israel's successful revolt against the Roman dogs, he had brought shame, disgrace and dishonor upon himself and his family. Better if he had never been born!

Never been born; maybe that was the answer. Life had lost its purpose and its meaning. Perhaps it was time to face the final futility — or the futile finality. Judas bought some rope and trudged eastward down a dirty Jerusalem street.

His body was later found hanging from the limbs of a tree just outside Jerusalem.

Via Dolorosa

The crucifixion detail stripped the royal robes from Jesus and put his own garments on him. Since his back had been thoroughly lacerated by the scourging, tearing the robes from his back caused his wounds to be ripped open again, which resulted in an additional loss of blood.

The soldiers placed the patibulum, or horizontal crossbar of the cross, across the nape of Jesus' neck, balanced it along both shoulders, and then tied his outstretched arms to it. Three other men had been previously condemned to be crucified, but one of those three—Barabbas—had been released to the Jewish mob by Pilate. Thus, Jesus was joined by the other two condemned men, each of whom carried his own patibulum to the place he would be executed. Four soldiers were assigned to each of the three convicts, and a contingent of Roman guards surrounded them. The entire crucifixion detail was under the command of the centurion Longinus. The Roman guard immediately in front of each condemned man carried that man's titulus, a sign on which the condemned man's name and crime were displayed. Anyone watching the procession would therefore know what crime the man had been convicted of committing. Later, the titulus would be attached to the top of the convict's cross.

Keeping pace with the soldiers was a group of women. Although their faces were largely hidden by veils, their grief could not be hidden. Some cried, while others prayed or moaned. One woman, who was clutching a small child, kept repeating over and over to anyone near enough to hear her, "How can they kill the man who healed my child?"

As the procession moved from the Praetorium along the Via Dolorosa toward the place where the crucifixion would take place, Jesus stumbled and fell. Since his arms were tied to the crossbar he carried, Jesus could not break his fall. His face slammed against the rough uneven stones paving the street. Blood trickled down Jesus' face from lacerations on his right cheek. One of the soldiers lashed him severely with a scourge. Longinus, however, directed two other soldiers to help lift the patibulum so that Jesus could stand under the load. As Jesus struggled to his feet, a middle-aged man rushed to his side and gave him a gourd of water before being knocked backward by one of the soldiers.

"What do you think you are doing?" shouted the Roman to the man.

"He cured my blindness," the man answered.

Twice more Jesus fell. He had lost a great deal of blood during his scourging and was in much worse condition than the other two convicts. The third time he fell, it was obvious to Longinus that the rabbi had lost too much blood to be able to continue carrying the patibulum—which weighed over a hundred pounds—by himself. Looking around, the centurion saw a man in the crowd who appeared to be rather strong, and whose dress indicated he was probably a Gentile.

"You," he said to the man. "Pick up that crossbar and carry it for this man."

"Me?" cried the stranger. "I have nothing to do with this affair. I was merely on my way into Jerusalem from Cyrene when my way was blocked by this throng of people."

"What is your name?"

"Simon. Please let me proceed on my way."

"Granted," Longinus said. "You may proceed on your way as soon as you have taken this patibulum to the top of that hill."

As two of the soldiers started toward Simon to help enforce the order, the Cyrene shrugged, handed a pack he had been carrying to one of his companions, and moved over to the place where Jesus lay. The soldiers untied the ropes that bound the patibulum to Jesus and laid it across Simon's shoulders. He then quickly carried the heavy wooden crossbar up the hill and dumped it onto the ground near the other two convicts and the rest of the soldiers. Then Simon briskly returned to his companions on the road and they proceeded into Jerusalem.

The hill where Jesus and the other two condemned men were crucified was called Golgotha.[15] It was Roman custom to perform the crucifixions outside the city walls, but close enough to both the walls and to major roads to be easily visible to large groups of people.

The vertical portion of the cross—the heavy upright wooden stipes, which would typically weigh about two hundred pounds— permanently remained at the site of execution. The crossbar would be attached to the stipes to form the cross of execution. If the executioners desired to prolong a person's death over several days, they might use ropes to tie the arms to the crossbar rather than using spikes, which would usually cause greater loss of blood and thus would hasten death. Since these three executions were being performed on the day before the Passover Sabbath, all three bodies would be required to be removed from the crosses before sundown to keep from offending Jewish religious customs and legal

[15] The Aramaic form of the Hebrew word meaning "the place of the skull." The Latin version is Calvary.

requirements. Therefore, all three men were nailed to their respective crosses.

The Roman soldiers attached the patibulum to the stipes, stripped Jesus' clothing from him[16], and set it aside. One of the soldiers roughly shoved Jesus to the ground, and two other soldiers positioned his body above the stipes, and then stretched out his arms above the patibulum. The fourth soldier in the detail pressed a knee against Jesus' right forearm and placed a tapered iron spike approximately six inches long next to Jesus' right wrist.

Jesus turned his head toward the man. He had once stilled a stormy sea by pointing to it with that same hand and commanding the storm to be still. That hand had pointed at Lazarus' tomb when he issued the command that raised the dead. That hand had mixed his saliva with dirt when he gave the gift of sight to a blind man. That hand had picked up a servant's ear when he healed the one who was arresting him at Gethsemane. But this time he did nothing to

---

[16] Romans stripped crucifixion victims to heighten their sense of shame.

stop the soldier from driving the spike through his wrist between the radius and the carpal bones.[17] Instead, Jesus merely writhed with pain as the spike pierced his skin, severed his sensorimotor median nerve, impaled his flexor pollicis longus, and then anchored his arm to the wooden crossbar.

After both arms had been nailed to the patibulum, both Jesus and the cross to which he was nailed were lifted up. Jesus' cry of agony mixed with the jarring thud of the cross as the stipes fell into the hole that had been prepared for it. Since Jesus' two companions had been nailed to their respective crossbars while Simon was carrying Jesus' patibulum up Golgotha, they were crucified on the shorter or lower Tau crosses, so called because they were shaped like that Greek letter (T). However, the cross in the center was the higher immissa or Latin cross. After Jesus was hanging from his cross, his

---

[17] By placing the nail between either the radius and the carpal bones or between the two rows of carpal bones, the spike would not fracture any bones and would permit the victim's skeleton to support his weight during the crucifixion. It should also be noted that people at that point in time customarily considered the wrist to be part of the hand.

ankles were squeezed sideways into a small U-shaped wooden block, which was then nailed to the stipes in such a manner that the nails were driven through Jesus' heels, securing the block to the cross. The soldiers then drove wedges between the beam and the sides of the hole to keep the cross fully upright.

After the nailing had been completed, the titulus was attached to the cross right above the condemned man's head. Pilate had instructed that Jesus' titulus should be inscribed in Hebrew, Latin and Greek as "Jesus of Nazareth, the King of the Jews." When the chief priests saw the titulus, they complained bitterly to Pilate, "Do not write 'The King of the Jews'; Instead, write 'This man said, "I am King of the Jews."'"

Pilate answered forcefully, "What I have written, I have written," and refused to change the wording on Jesus' titulus. Although the words correctly stated the charge for which Jesus was being executed, Pilate may have intended the message to mock the jealous Jewish leaders or to warn other persons with kingly aspirations of Rome's likely response. In any event, the message that Jesus was "King of the Jews" was conveyed in the language of Jewish religion and history, the language of Roman law and government, and the language of Greek culture.

When the soldiers had nailed Jesus to the cross, they took his garments and divided them so that each would have one item. However, since his tunic was seamless, woven in one piece from top to bottom, they decided to cast lots for it to see whose it should be.

By law, the condemned man was normally given a bitter drink of wine mixed with myrrh or gall as a mild analgesic. Jesus, however, refused to take any drug that would deaden his pain or reduce his consciousness.

Crucifixion

Longinus was intrigued by the man hanging on the center cross. It had been his duty to observe Jesus several times over the past couple of years. He had heard Jesus preach his message of forgiveness and compassion; he could probably recite verbatim what Jesus would say about God's grace and mercy. But Longinus was curious about how such platitudes would measure up against the realities of crucifixion.

The centurion was no stranger to crucifixions. He was accustomed to being cursed and reviled by men hanging on crosses. Rage, hostility and threats of retaliation were common. Even notorious murderers would claim to be innocent and would curse both their accusers and their executioners.

Jesus, however, showed none of those emotions. Granted, he did cry out in agony when the cross fell into its hole with a resounding thud—but that cry was not accompanied with the vindictive verbiage that streamed from the other two crosses.

Longinus looked at all three men. Although their arms had been stretched out in virtually straight lines when they were being nailed to their crosses, the weight of their bodies and the ripping of their flesh had caused their arms to form V positions. Both shoulders were dislocated. When Jesus' bones were ripped out of their joints, his arms stretched and were lengthened by approximately six inches.

All three men moaned at the almost unbearable pain in their wrists, and all three attempted to flex their muscles to relieve the severe cramping that knotted their forearms and the pads of their shoulders. It was plain that all three convicts were suffering, but only the two known by Longinus to be guilty of insurrection were bitterly complaining about their fate.

When the soldiers finished stabilizing the crosses by driving wedges of wood around the bases, the perimeter guards stepped back and allowed the onlookers to approach the spectacle. The mob that had been demanding Jesus' crucifixion pressed forward to get a better look at their victim. Faces leered up at the teacher who was now suspended above them. Fingers pointed to the man who had calmed raging storms but now seemed helpless and humbled. Snarling faces convulsed as they taunted him, wagged their heads, and gloated.

"Not so all-powerful now, are you, Jesus?" Matthias jeered. "You, who would destroy the temple and build it again in three days, save yourself! If you really are the Son of God, come down from the cross!"

A Pharisee named Saul hugged Matthias and exulted, "We got him! Despite everything, we finally succeeded in bringing him down." Saul then joined in the mockery by motioning toward Jesus while jeering, "He saved others, but he cannot save himself." The chief priests, scribes and elders laughed and repeated the taunt.

Caiaphas turned to his colleagues and loudly intoned, "He claimed to be the Messiah—the King of Israel! Let him now come down from the cross, and we will believe him. Since he trusts in God, let the Lord rescue him—provided, of course, that God really cares anything about him. After all, he claimed that he was the Son of God!"

Longinus studied the faces of the men who were reviling Jesus, and then turned to look at the rabbi nailed to the cross. The difference startled the centurion. The religious leaders reminded him of a band of demons celebrating the demise of a hated enemy, while the man on the cross looked sad and sympathetic.

The crowd's jeering was so loud that only those standing near Jesus' cross heard him quietly pray, "Father, forgive them, for they know not what they do."

Longinus closely studied Jesus' face as he spoke. *I think he's serious. He really* is *praying for his enemies—not for their condemnation and death, but rather for their forgiveness and salvation. How often have I seen crucified men pray for their god to rain vengeance upon the heads of their enemies — but never have I heard something like this!*

If I had been convicted of a crime I didn't commit, could I pray for my accusers? If I had been nailed to a cross, could I pray for the jealous leaders who had put me there? I had heard him teaching that we should pray for our enemies, but dismissed those statements as being impractical platitudes that could never happen. But he's actually doing it!

Longinus snapped out of his thoughtful reverie as he became aware that his soldiers had joined the crowd in mocking Jesus, coming up to him and offering him vinegar, and saying, "If you really are the King of the Jews, save yourself!"

One of the criminals being executed alongside Jesus yelled to him, "Yeah, if you really are the Messiah, save yourself — and us!"

However, the other condemned man rebuked the first one by saying, "Don't you even fear God — you who are receiving the same punishment? You and I fully deserve the punishment we are getting for what we did. But this man has done nothing wrong." Then he turned as far as he could toward Jesus and pleaded, "Lord Jesus, please remember me when you come into your kingdom."

"I tell you truly," Jesus replied through lips that were cracked and swollen, "today you will be with me in paradise."

*****

Standing near the cross was a group of grieving women, including Jesus' mother. Mary thought back to Gabriel's announcement that she had been chosen by God to bear the Christ child—the promised Messiah who would save his people. She had willingly allowed herself to be used for God's mission, even though it meant people would spread rumors about her and talk about how she had been unfaithful to Joseph. When he had taken her as his wife anyway, the gossip had changed to make him a party to the shame of not waiting until marriage to be intimate with each other. When they had returned to Nazareth after Jesus' birth, the gossipers resumed making their snide remarks.

It had not been an easy life, but Mary had willingly and even joyfully done her part. However, seeing her son nailed to a cruel cross, broken and bleeding, eyes puffy and body covered with caked blood, was more than she could bear. Making it even worse were the gloating, mocking and derisive insults being hurled at her son by the people who surrounded the crosses. They were nothing but a pack of jackals!

God had promised Mary that the child she bore would be the long-anticipated Messiah who would save his people. She had always believed that God was trustworthy and kept his promises. *If that is true, then how can it end this way? Jesus never hurt anyone. He spent his entire life helping and healing, encouraging and lifting people up. Where is God's justice in allowing these jackals to treat him this way? How does this fulfill Gabriel's promise? What is the purpose? God, how can you let this happen?*

*****

Standing next to Mary was Mary Magdalene, whose life had quite literally been transformed by Jesus. Once she had vainly sought to find meaning in life by looking in all the wrong places. Because she was unusually attractive and naturally seductive, she had numerous men who showered her with attention and material possessions. But the odd thing was that the more she got what she thought she wanted, the more miserable she felt. Just when she thought life had no meaning, she met Jesus—and he almost magically rid her of the demons that were tormenting her.

Mary Magdalene had followed Jesus ever since. He was different from any other man she had ever known. Although she had initially attempted to flirt with him, Jesus seemed impervious to her seductive powers and seemed only concerned with her spiritual relationship with God. However, being around Jesus and learning from his teaching had given purpose and meaning to her life. Until now. Seeing the most wonderful person she had ever known suspended between heaven and earth on a Roman cross was causing her mind to spin out of control. Knowing that he would soon be dead was even worse. And those jeering, leering maniacs taunting Jesus really caused her blood to boil!

It just isn't right! God, where is your justice? How can you let this happen? The great physician shouldn't die; the good shepherd should still be caring for his flock. Her eyes filled with tears as she clung to Jesus' mother and to the "other" Mary—the one who was the wife of Clopas—for support. All three Marys cried, averting their eyes at times because it was so painful to watch Jesus hanging in agony.

*****

When Jesus saw his mother standing near his disciple John, he said to her, "Woman, behold your son," and tilted his head toward John. Then he said to John, "Behold your mother."

John gasped as he realized the implications. Although it would have been customary for Mary's other children to look after her once Jesus was no longer able to do so, he was passing his mantle as eldest son to his beloved disciple. In so doing, Jesus was entrusting her care to John. The disciple silently nodded, signaling his willingness to take Mary into his own home and care for her.

*****

Longinus shook his head and marveled to himself, *Even as this man is struggling for breath while dying on a cross, he still is primarily concerned for the welfare of others!*

Although the pain involved in a crucifixion is quite literally excruciating,[18] the actual cause of death is a long, slow, agonizing suffocation caused by the body's inability to perform normal respiration and exhalation.[19] In order to perform anything approximating normal breathing, Jesus had to push himself upward and fight for his breath, even though such a maneuver produced searing pain. Pushing up caused the nail to tear through his foot,

---

[18] "Excruciating" is a term that means "of or from the cross."

[19] The weight of the body pulling down on the outstretched arms and shoulders locked Jesus' intercostal muscles in an inhalation position that caused him to almost be unable to exhale. Although crucifixion caused the victim's body to experience hypovolemic shock, dehydration, stress-induced heart arrhythmias, and congestive heart failure, the actual cause of death was normally asphyxiation, which occurred when the victim's exhausted body gave out and he could no longer push up for breath.

eventually locking up against the tarsal bones, and scraped his blooded and pulverized back against the coarse wood of the cross. He could then take several rapid breaths before letting his body relax as he hung by his wrists for a few moments before pushing back up again for more breath.

Beginning around noon, a strange and unnatural darkness covered the land for approximately three hours. The uncanny darkness at this time of day had a sobering effect upon the crowd. The jeers faded into silence, and the mob began to disperse.

*****

At least two of the Jewish religious leaders who watched Jesus' execution did not join in the mockery, jeering and celebrations. Rather, they stood off by themselves in stunned silence as the man they had hoped was the promised Messiah was nailed to the cross and as he slowly died.

"I really believed that he was the Messiah," said Joseph of Arimathea sorrowfully.

"I hadn't come to that conclusion," Nicodemus responded, "but I had pretty well concluded that he was the Son of God, since the evidence we found indicated that God Almighty had used a part of his own pure energy or spirit to impregnate Mary. However, if Jesus dies, that should show conclusively that he could not be partially God or even the Son of God."

"Why is that?" Joseph asked.

"Well, since God is eternal, he obviously cannot die. Therefore, if Jesus dies, he could not be God or even the Son of God."

"Couldn't the same thing be said about the Messiah?" asked Joseph. "Since the Messiah is supposed to sit on the throne of David and rule our people forever, he would have to be alive for that to occur. Thus, if he dies, he could not reign as Messiah."

"You are probably correct, Joseph. Indeed, I think you are right. Dying would show that he is not the Messiah and is not the Son of God."

"Then both of us have been mistaken about Jesus and who he really is."

"So it would seem, Joseph. So it would seem."

The two men were quiet for several minutes. Then Joseph announced, "Well, I have decided to act on the last portion of Jesus' prayer for us that night we met with him."

"What do you mean?"

"Jesus prayed that you and I would have the courage to do what was right."

"I remember—but just what do you have in mind?"

"It appears unlikely to me that any miraculous event is going to occur that will save Jesus from death on the cross. If God were going to send the armies of heaven to intervene, I don't think he would have sent this darkness that has now lasted for over an hour. No, I think Jesus is going to die. But he doesn't have to die as a common criminal whose body will be tossed on a refuse pile or burned. I have decided that what is right would be to provide a decent burial for him."

"What?" asked Nicodemus incredulously. "All this time that you were hoping or even possibly believing he was the Messiah, you've been too afraid of our comrades on the Sanhedrin to declare to anyone other than me what you thought. Now that you know he is not the Messiah, you decide to openly show your support for him by giving him a proper burial? Am I hearing you correctly?"

"It does sound crazy, doesn't it?" Joseph remarked. "Nevertheless, I am convinced that it is the right and proper thing to do."

"Let me point out something else," Nicodemus added. "In addition to possibly alienating our friends and associates among the Jewish religious hierarchy, touching a dead body will render you unclean for the entire Passover celebration—one of the most important events of our year. In fact, it will mean you would be ceremonially unclean for seven full days."

"Perhaps that is why it will take courage to do what is right in this situation."

"It's madness, man. Do you realize all the things that must be done in order to carry out such an assignment—and how little time you have to get it done?"

"Yes, I think I do know, Nicodemus. As soon as Jesus dies, I must go to Pilate and request that his body be turned over to me. I would also need to procure the long linen burial cloth as well as the spices that must be wrapped in that cloth in order to offset the smell of the decaying body."

"That's just the beginning. Where would you put the body? Remember, everything must be completed before the Sabbath begins at six o'clock this evening."

"That's the easy part. I can use my own tomb. It is only a short distance from here."

"But that is your personal tomb for you and your family. You could never use it once a convicted criminal's body has been placed inside it."

"I know, but I am convinced that this is what is right and is what needs to be done for Jesus. Will you join me?"

"I—I don't know, Joseph. You know how hard I have worked to become recognized as Israel's master teacher of the law, don't you? I could be throwing all that away by joining you in this one reckless act."

"Yes, Nicodemus, I know. As I said earlier, it would require courage to do what is right. Prayerfully consider whether such an action is also right for you. You may join me if you wish, or I will do it alone. The choice is yours. But don't delay too long. We don't have much time. I am going to go to my shipping office to round up some men to assist me. If you wish to help, then purchase the linen and burial spices. I'll be back here as soon as I gather my men. And cheer up. Perhaps God will still send a few legions of his angels to save Jesus from the cross, and none of our actions and preparations will be needed." With that, Joseph trotted back down the road that led to Jerusalem. Nicodemus sank to his knees and earnestly prayed.

*****

During this time of darkness, Jesus felt the overwhelming weight of the sins of mankind being pressed against his soul—a feeling even more horrible than the excruciating pain of physical crucifixion. Though he had never sinned, he felt the shame and disgrace of sinners. He who had never murdered, stolen, committed adultery or lied now felt the embarrassment and shame felt by murderers, thieves, adulterers and liars. Since he bore the sins of the world, he felt the collective shame of a world of sinners.

Just as agonizing for him, however, was the terrible loneliness he felt as he was separated from the sustaining presence of divine support. That was worse than the pain of the spikes, worse than the agony of pushing up to get breath, and worse than the irritation of the flies, gnats, and other insects that were attracted to the battered and bleeding bodies nailed to rough crosses.

About three o'clock in the afternoon, Jesus arched his back, straining against the spikes that held him to the cross, tilted his head upward and cried with a loud voice to heaven above, "My God, my God, why have you forsaken me?" Jesus had reached the point where he was the perfect sacrifice for a world of sinners. As if in response to his question, the darkness abated and light returned to the land.

Jesus then looked around and said, "I thirst!"

One of the soldiers took a sponge, filled it with vinegar, stuck it on a reed, and held it up to Jesus' mouth for him to drink. When Jesus had done so, he took a deep breath as he pushed up one final time, and shouted triumphantly, "*Tetelestai!*[20] It is finished! Father, into your hands I commit my spirit." Jesus then bowed his head, stopped pushing up for breath, and died.

A sudden earthquake shook the land, splitting rocks and opening tombs. Shock waves were felt in the temple. Several priests were in the temple's inner chamber[21] when they heard a loud ripping noise. As they watched, the extremely thick, elaborate and strong inner veil[22] of the temple was torn in two, from top to bottom.

---

[20] *Tetelestai* was a Greek accounting term meaning that a debt had been paid in full. In this case Jesus was declaring that the debt for mankind's sin had been paid in full, the ledger had been balanced, and nothing else is required to be paid.

[21] Only priests were allowed to enter this chamber, which was known as the Holy Place.

[22] The *katapetasma* was sixty feet long, thirty feet wide, and as thick as the palm of a man's hand; it separated the Holy Place from the Holy of Holies.

"What in the world?" cried one priest.

"That's impossible!" exclaimed another. "Not even teams of oxen could pull apart that curtain!"

"Oh, my God! Look! We can see into the Holy of Holies itself," said a third priest as he sank to his knees and then fell face down on the floor. "Pray that we aren't struck dead for seeing what only the high priest is allowed to see—and he can only do it on the Day of Atonement."

The other priests looked at each other in alarm, and then they also quickly prostrated themselves and prayed earnestly.

*****

The centurion Longinus and his soldiers had initially been intrigued by Jesus' lack of the emotions they had come to expect at crucifixions; there was no rage, fear, anger, hostility, cursing or threats of retaliation. Instead, they witnessed Jesus' kindness and compassion as he hung on the cross—and they observed with awe the prolonged three-hour darkness during what should have been the brightest part of the day. The darkness had ended immediately before Jesus' final comments, declaration of victorious accomplishment of his mission, and death, and was followed immediately thereafter by the earthquake.

Longinus knelt down and reverently exclaimed, "Surely this man really was the Son of God!"

When the people in the crowd who had gathered to see the spectacle saw what had happened, they returned home confused as to what they had witnessed—and what it all meant. Jesus' friends and the women who had followed him from Galilee stood at a distance from the crosses, but watched all these things from that vantage point.

Because the law of Moses does not allow bodies to remain on crosses on the Sabbath, the Jews had asked Pilate to have the criminals' legs broken and then have the bodies disposed of so that they would not remain hanging between heaven and earth on the Sabbath. Breaking the legs would cause almost immediate death, of course, since the victim could no longer push up for breath. The soldiers therefore broke the legs of the men crucified with Jesus. Since Jesus was already dead, they did not break his. Nevertheless, one of the soldiers pierced Jesus' side with a spear, perforating his right lung, pericardium and heart. Blood and water immediately flowed out, satisfying the Roman soldiers that Jesus was truly dead.[23]

---

[23] Jesus' hypovolemic shock would have caused a sustained rapid heart rate, which in turn led to heart failure and resulted in the collection of fluid in the membrane around the heart and lungs, which is called pericardial effusion and pleural effusion, respectively. When the soldier's spear was pulled out of Jesus' body, the clear fluid or effusion came out, followed by a large volume of blood.

Burial

Shortly before the middle of the afternoon, Joseph returned to Golgotha with a contingent of his men. He did not see Nicodemus, but watched the events that unfolded that day. As soon as Longinus officially pronounced Jesus to be dead, Joseph and one of his servants rode into Jerusalem on horseback. He went directly to Pilate's quarters in the Praetorium and sought audience with the governor.

Pilate was shocked to see a Jewish Pharisee and member of the Great Sanhedrin in the Roman structure. "I thought you Jews couldn't enter this building without becoming defiled," Pilate remarked.

"If you grant my request, I will be worse than defiled," Joseph answered.

"Sounds interesting. What is your request?"

"Your Excellency, I request permission to

take the body of Jesus of Nazareth so that it may be given a proper burial."

"Is he already dead?"

"Yes, your Excellency. You may verify his death with your crucifixion detail."

"I'll do that." Pilate turned to one of his guards and said, "Go with this man to Calvary and speak to the centurion Longinus. If Jesus is truly dead, release his body to this man. That will be one fewer corpse to dispose of. And tell Longinus that when he returns from Calvary, I want a full report about both the crucifixion and the mob that demanded Jesus' execution."

When they got back to Golgotha, Longinus confirmed that Jesus was dead, and the body was removed from the cross by the Roman soldiers and granted to Joseph, who had his men transport it to Joseph's own new tomb cut in the rock in a nearby garden, and in which no one had yet been laid. Nicodemus also returned with about seventy-five pounds' weight of myrrh, aloe and similar burial spices.

They took Jesus' body and flexed and massaged his arms to relieve the rigor mortis that had fixed his arms in the V position. Then they washed his body in accordance with Jewish law and custom, bound it in linen winding cloths along with the spices, also according to the burial custom of the Jews, and laid it in Joseph's tomb. A separate napkin tied under Jesus' chin kept his mouth from opening wide as his muscles loosened.

They then rolled the large disk-shaped stone known as the Golel[24] along its curved notch so that it firmly blocked the entrance to the tomb. Jewish law required everything to be completed before sundown.[25]

The next day, the chief priests and a group of Pharisees gathered before Pilate and said, "Sir, we remember that while he was still alive, that imposter and deceiver, Jesus of Nazareth, said that he would rise again on the third day. Therefore, we ask you to command that Jesus'

---

[24] Golel means "great stone."

[25] Not only must they complete all work prior to the Sabbath (which began at sundown), but Deuteronomy 21:22-23 says, "If a man guilty of a capital offense is put to death and his body is hung on a tree, you must not leave his body on the tree overnight. Be sure to bury him that same day, because anyone who is hung on a tree is under God's curse."

tomb be made secure until after the third day, lest his disciples come and steal his body away and claim to the people that he has indeed risen from the dead. If that were allowed to happen, this last fraud would be worse than any of the others."

"You shall have a guard," Pilate responded. "In addition to the guard I post, you may also use your own guard to make it as secure as you can."

Thus it was that the Jewish religious leaders—whose chief complaints about Jesus tended to be that he healed people on the Sabbath rather than observing their rules and regulations not to do any work on that day—gathered together temple guards and posted them around the tomb of Jesus *on the Sabbath*—and not just any Sabbath, but on the high day of the Passover Sabbath itself.

When the Roman guard assigned by Pilate arrived at Jesus' tomb, they first rolled aside the huge Golel that blocked the entrance. Because the stone weighed several tons and because it rested in the deep slanting groove that had been hewn out of the rock at the base of the entrance, such stones were extremely difficult to push back up the incline. Nevertheless, the soldiers did so, since they had been commanded to confirm that the body of Jesus was still in the tomb.

After the soldiers had confirmed that the body was there and that there were no other openings into the tomb, they rolled the Golel back into place and sealed the entrance by cementing it to the surrounding stone. The Roman soldiers then placed hardening clay across the stone and marked it with the seal of the emperor. Breaking such a seal would invite Roman retaliation and retribution. Then both the Roman and the Jewish temple guards took their positions around the tomb.

Other Books by Bill Kincaid

Historical Fiction:

Nicodemus' Quest—The Jewish Supreme Court known as the Sanhedrin had already found Jesus Christ guilty of blasphemy and condemned him to die, setting in motion the events culminating in his death by crucifixion a few hours later. Why then would two of the most influential members of the Sanhedrin risk alienating their colleagues by removing Jesus' body from the cross and giving him a proper burial? Didn't they realize it was a lost cause—that Jesus' death proved he couldn't be either the Messiah or the son of God?

Yet Nicodemus and Joseph of Arimathea risked everything they had worked so hard for throughout their lives by identifying with Jesus at a time when even his friends and disciples had deserted him. What had they learned in their investigations into Jesus' background and ministry that caused them to take such drastic action? For that matter, why had they investigated him in the first place? Is Jesus the Messiah—and what relevance does that have for us two thousand years later?

Saul's Quest—Saul of Tarsus appeared to have an extremely bright future. He had distinguished himself as being the star pupil of Gamaliel, who was considered the outstanding first century teacher in Israel. Although still a young man, Saul had already been accepted as a member of both the Pharisees and of the Sanhedrin, the principal legislative and judicial body of Israel.

Now the Jewish high priest has given Saul the assignment of hunting down, arresting, and persecuting the men and women who claim that Jesus of Nazareth is both the Messiah and the Son of God. Saul pursued the task with his usual dedication and determination . . . until something unusual happens on the road to Damascus. Walk with Saul on his momentous journey that radically changed not only his life, but also the history of the world.

Science Fiction / Fantasy

Wizard's Gambit— Out of the thousands of planets searched by unmanned space probes, sixteen have both water and an atmosphere similar enough to Earth's to make colonization feasible. These planets have been listed as being Earth Virtual Equivalents—or EVEs.

On Eve Twelve—one of only three planets to have water in a liquid state each time the it was checked by probes–a power struggle is developing that could have far-reaching consequences, the ripples from which could even reach and impact Earth.

Wizard's Gambit tells the story of that conflict—and more—as good and evil wizards pit technology against magic in a battle for supremacy of a planet populated by both people and dragons.

[Available 2017]

Fractured Fairy Tale:
Ronald Raygun and the Sweeping Beauty~

COLE BLACK RAYGUN might be a well respected king, but he still had a problem. Yes, it's true old King Cole had a reputation for being a merry old soul, but at the moment he was definitely not feeling particularly merry. Frustrated would be a more accurate word. Frustrated by that stubborn and obstinate son of his!

Although Crown Prince Ronald Raygun was heir apparent to the throne, it was not at all apparent who his bride—the future queen—would be. Ronald had never met a girl he liked enough to date more than a few times, much less to consider marrying. And old King Cole desperately wanted to spoil some grandchildren before he died. Luckily, King Cole can call upon the services of his Royal Attorney, Lord Shyster, who helps him find the necessary Royal Loopholes in the law that requires royalty to only marry other royalty or nobility . . .

Although this fractured fairy tale primarily satirizes the classic *Cinderella* tale, it also manages to fracture *Sleeping Beauty* and *The Princess and the Pea*—while also having fun with various politicians and other celebrities. But are you astute enough to catch all the hidden meanings and references?

All titles are available on Amazon.com and Kindle.